W9-AGO-384

Cranes

by M. T. Martin

Content Consultant:
Robert I. Carr, PhD, PE

BELLWETHER MEDIA • MINNEAPOLIS, MN

Note to Librarians, Teachers, and Parents:

Blastoff! Readers are carefully developed by literacy experts and combine standards-based content with developmentally appropriate text.

Level 1 provides the most support through repetition of high-frequency words, light text, predictable sentence patterns, and strong visual support.

Level 2 offers early readers a bit more challenge through varied simple sentences, increased text load, and less repetition of high-frequency words.

Level 3 advances early-fluent readers toward fluency through increased text and concept load, less reliance on visuals, longer sentences, and more literary language.

Whichever book is right for your reader, Blastoff! Readers are the perfect books to build confidence and encourage a love of reading that will last a lifetime!

This edition first published in 2007 by Bellwether Media.

No part of this publication may be reproduced in whole or in part without written permission of the publisher. For information regarding permission, write to Bellwether Media Inc., Attention: Permissions Department, Post Office Box 1C, Minnetonka, MN 55345-9998.

Library of Congress Cataloging-in-Publication Data
Martin, M. T. (Martin Theodore)
  Cranes / by M. T. Martin.
    p. cm. — (Blastoff! readers) (Mighty machines)
Summary: "Simple text and supportive images introduce young readers to cranes. Intended for students in kindergarten through third grade."
  Includes bibliographical references and index.
  ISBN-10: 1-60014-045-9 (hardcover : alk. paper)
  ISBN-13: 978-1-60014-045-7 (hardcover : alk. paper)
  1. Cranes, derricks, etc.—Juvenile literature. I. Title. II. Series. III. Series: Mighty machines (Bellwether Media)
  TJ1363.M288 2006
  621.8'73—dc22   2006007213

Text copyright © 2007 by Bellwether Media.
Printed in the United States of America.

Table of Contents

What Is a Crane?   4

Parts of a Crane   8

The Crane at Work   18

Glossary   20

To Learn More   23

Index   24

Cranes are the tallest machines at a **work site**.

Cranes lift
and move
heavy **loads**.

This crane has
a **boom** and **hook**.
Some cranes have
a shovel or bucket.

boom

hook

Some cranes
have wheels.
They move from
place to place.

Tower cranes
do not move.
They sit on bases.

A crane has a **cab**. A worker sits in the cab.

cab

The worker
pushes pedals
and pulls levers
to move the crane.

Cranes
lift **cargo**
off ships.

Cranes help build
tall bridges.
Can you think
of other things
cranes build?

Glossary

boom—a long metal arm

cab—a place for the driver to sit

cargo—loads carried by ship, train, or truck

hook—a curved piece of metal used for catching, holding, or pulling

load—anything that is carried or lifted by a machine or a person

tower cranes—the tallest cranes; they do not have wheels.

work site—a place where construction takes place

To Learn More

AT THE LIBRARY

Gore, Bryson. *Trucks, Tractors, and Cranes.*
Brookfield, Conn.: Copper Beech Books, 2000.

Granowsky, Alvin. *Diggers and Cranes.*
Brookfield, Conn.: Copper Beech Books, 2000.

Randolph, Joanne. *Cranes.* New York:
Powerkids Press, 2002.

ON THE WEB

Learning more about mighty
machines is as easy as 1, 2, 3.

1. Go to www.factsurfer.com

2. Enter "mighty machines" into search box.

3. Click the "Surf" button and you will see a list
   of related web sites.

With factsurfer.com, finding more information is
just a click away.

Index

bases, 12

boom, 8

bridges, 20

cab, 14

cargo, 18

hook, 8

loads, 6

tower cranes, 12

wheels, 10

work site, 4

The photographs in this book are reproduced with the permission of: R.I Carr, front cover, pp. 5, 17; GJS, p. 7; Johnny Lye, p. 9; Jo Lin, p. 11; Daniel Gale, p. 13; Roman Levin, p. 15; Bertrand Collet, p. 19; Alex Maclean/Getty Images, p. 21.